An Invocation of Fragments

An Invocation of Fragments

Poems by Ted Charnley

Cover design by Shay Culligan
Cover art by Sir Lawrence Alma-Tadema,
Sappho and Alcaeus, 1881

ISBN: 978-1-63980-143-5

Kelsay Books
502 South 1040 East, A-119
American Fork, Utah 84003
Kelsaybooks.com

Acknowledgments

Able Muse Review: "The Rape of Proserpina"

Blue Unicorn: "As He Is to Us"

The Lyric: "Life as a Boneless Chicken," "They're Here to Protect You (From the Bogeyman)," "Lights on the Dashboard" and "They're Not Wearing Capes"

The Orchards Poetry Journal: "A Service Economy," "Just a Rondeau for Cassandra," "For Lady Macbeth, in the 21st Century," "Damaged Goods" and "The Clepsydra"

Passager: "At the Museum of the Book" and "Cacophony in Concert"

The Road Not Taken: "Orrery," "Lyrics From a Distance" and "The Sentry"

Slant: "Once and Future Kings" and "Bourbon and Bienville"

Think: "Cinderella in Reverse" and "The Boomer Is Put Out to Pasture"

Extreme Sonnets: "At the Museum of the Book," "Damaged Goods" and "Lyrics From a Distance"

Extreme Formal Poems: "For Lady Macbeth, in the 21st Century," "Just a Rondeau for Cassandra," "Once and Future Kings" and "They're Here to Protect You (From the Bogeyman)"

"An Invocation of Fragments" was selected as a finalist for the 2019 Frost Farm Prize for Metrical Poetry (Bruce Bennett judging), and received honorable mention for the 2020 Able Muse Write Prize (Emily Grosholz judging). "As He Is to Us" was nominated for a 2021 Pushcart Prize.

To Anne Marie, for her patience and generosity,

To Bruce, for his perceptiveness

And to Barb, for her tolerance of it all.

Contents

III. Stories That Mothers Tell

Front cover: "Sappho and Alcaeus" by Sir Lawrence Alma-Tadema (Dutch and British), 1881.

An Invocation of Fragments

Sappho, please; please come to me not with anger,
not to Anaktoria, not to Atthis.
Tenth of sisters numbering nine, come dark-haired,
sultry, petite one.

I, who call you back to the *Kallisteia*,
sing of you; you sang of me there. We played on
girls as strings on kitharas plucked, enjoyed such
pleasures together.

Now, our Cleïs binds us as daughter, calling
you from other arms to my own. We've made our
music where we found it, but you're the tone to
balance this triad.

Sappho, please; please silence iambic noises
wafting up on westerly winds, and turn them
back. Embrace my dactyls with yours; we'll hold one
stylus together.

Halls in Alexandria burn, papyrus
fails before your verse, but your name resounds. Come,
visit: I, Alkaios, implore you please-ing,
sweet-smiling Sappho.

No; one fragment cannot restore another.
Age has left us fallen estranged, as pieces
torn and scattered. Edges between them fit, yet
never complete us.

I.   Fragments

"When the sixteenth-century Dutch humanist Erasmus
translated [Works and Days] he confused the Greek word for
jar, pithos, with the word for box, pyxos; . . . but 'box' loses
important elements of the Greek word that make the jar,
rounded in shape and made of clay, a metonymy
for Pandora herself."

— Hesiod. *Works and Days*. C. Schlegel and H. Weinfield, Trans. Notes, 93.

Epimethiana
(Or Hindsight with Double Vision)

Remember, I, your brother, told you so,
and thought ahead to caution you
against accepting gifts from strangers, but
you want a fire, you get a woman.
She is pretty nice,
for clay
with an extreme makeover, now a gift.
You want the woman, you get some fruit,
but that's another story.
You want the woman, you get
her jar, and it is pretty
nice, all full and rounded like
her body, clay.
You want the jar, you get its contents, too.
With opened lids,
your eyes see good and ill,
but that's another story again.
You want the jar, you get
her opening the lid, and ills escape
for good; it's not so pretty nice,
whichever way it's told, what name she's called.
You want a plan, you've got no plan,
and now there's only hope that's left inside.
For soon the gift that keeps on
nagging for a bigger fire,

the jar not emptied yet, will see you
naked, ashamed, afraid
you're only clay;
again, that other story, looking back.
You want a plan, you've gotten
her with child; your only hope
her gift that keeps you, either way,
despite your own titanic
fall, immortal by descent.
For what you want, you get
cast out together, in another story
starting with some clay.

The Rape of Proserpina

I am Bernini, prodigy of Rome,
and she my helpless nymph and he my god.
I freed them from a single quarried block,
for her to flee, be caught and carried off.
Now see him lift her, see his grasping hand
compress the polished marble of her thigh.
She struggles, throwing back her head to scream
in vain, for I have given her no voice.

I am Bernini, bringing life to stone,
and she the wife of my assistant here
has modeled every detail, every line,
the fleshy thigh my grasping hand compressed.
She struggled, throwing back her head to scream
in vain, for I had given her no voice;
her husband needed work to keep them fed,
my scudi made him deaf, he looked away.

I am Bernini, favored by the Pope,
and with commissions from Borghese still.
They, too, will look away, for each of us
pursues his sculpted lust, his fleeing nymph.
But she, my shamed adulteress, will be jailed
the way we always take Proserpina;
we've given her no voice, she's carried off.
I am her Pluto, bringing stone to life.

"Please accept my resignation. I don't care to belong
to any club that will accept me as a member."
- Groucho Marx

Groucho Plays Narcissus

You bet your life I wouldn't ever join
a club that would accept me as a member;
so, if you want me, I don't want you,
although I did before. I'm sure there must
be something wrong with someone wanting me.

Just say the secret word, not sounds you heard
that end my lines; I'm bored by all your rhymes.
You see, you're one of those who got too close
to be a club I'd join. But up till then,
you really did appeal; please go away.

This story has its echoes, then divorce,
for I've resigned as member several times.
As with the nymphs I've met, the trick is not
to join a club; it's letting one join me.

Lyrics From a Distance

It makes you cry out loud, her violin;
the notes without a voice, the keening strings.
They almost rise and soar, she almost sings
to you among the crowd, then reels it in.

You want her closer now, to hear your words
accompany her music, if you can.
But when the encore ends, you're just a fan
who wants to meet her backstage afterwards.

And there, with all your knocking on her door,
you'll stand before her, tense, and try to read,
your starstruck words a stutter, nothing more.

Her face will blur, her knowing smile recede;
then, from afar, your lyrics rise and soar.
It isn't what you want, it's what you need.

Orrery

I was the Earl of Orrery and thus
the lord of my estates, ascended from
a shipwreck found off Antikythera.

And you, my moon, were lured and overcome
by slow and grave attractions, tighter orbits.
Lording my estates, ascending from

my place, I whirled in geocentric order.
Quietly, some clockwork gears would turn
to other grave attractions, wider orbits

go elliptic. Arms of bronze and iron
no longer hold the space between us true.
And you escape, as clockwork gears still turn

till I (around whom all revolve but you)
am not your earth, but just a distant sun.
So nothing holds the space between us true

when ancient models rust and come undone.
I was the Earl of Orrery and thus
your earth, I thought, not just a distant sun
or relic found off Antikythera.

Mithradates VII

If Mithradates took his poison daily,
smaller doses making ready for
the meds prescribed by his Laodice,
then I can take whatever you've in store.

If smaller doses make me ready for
the long and longer times I'm derelict,
then I can take whatever you've in store,
in patient tolerance of arsenic.

The long and longer times I'm derelict
have left me reading venom in your note;
impatient, tolerant of arsenic,
but running out of any antidote.

I'm leaving, reads the venom in your note
(with months of measured spoonfuls concentrated),
running out with all the antidote.
If now at once you have accumulated

months of measured spoonfuls, concentrated
here, then your prescription is *Take this*.
Now all at once you have accumulated
bitter strychnine out of pills, dismissed

me with it. Your prescription is *Take this
and this*. A final portion offers me
the bitter strychnine from your pills, dismissing
any chance to build immunity.

If this, the final portion offered me,
is prepped to flex my muscles into stone
without a chance to build immunity,
you've chosen someone, then, to take my throne.

Unprepped, no muscles flex what's cast in stone
with meds prescribed by you, Laodice.
Your chosen someone takes not just a throne;
each Mithradates takes your poison daily.

The Tale of the Late 5th Husband of the Wife of Bath

She lies! She lies! Tales that she tells of me,
the blow that deafened her ear, dealt for damage
done to my book – barefaced lies that I brooked.
The ear she turned was the ear I earned, surely
hurt by my distance, not my hand. Indeed,
my studies stilled my voice and stirred her anger.
Lo, when like the low-pitched thunder I spoke,
beneath her heed, she heard just hum or rumble.
She and her girls would thrill to gossip, though,
and never need or want a word repeated.

Some wife she was, bargaining leave for love
to pay her debt, daunting with needs in number.
Hark! The ear I shunned was the ear she earned,
not one the bard would write, weaving her slander,
damning me as a mean and violent man.
He couldn't call her bawdy, old and bitter,
me a neglectful gull as groom – oh no!
We can't compare with partial tales so perfect.
Truth to tell, a marriage in full is two
who talk at length and turn an ear to listen.

Damaged Goods

On market day, my nag and I will pull
our aching selves and overburdened cart
to town, with foraged fruit and garden cull.
For there, among the peddlers taking part,
the jugglers, fools and passersby, I'll hawk
these apples, soft and fallen, scallions scorned,
these battered, stringy beans from trampled stalks,
this mildewed melon, gap-tooth ears of corn.

If just one shopper saw some value here
or stopped to bargain, she would find my fees
are low, my terms are easy. None comes near.
Once more tonight, my nag and I will feed
on foraged fruit and garden cull, our type
of damaged goods – the bruised and overripe.

Hestia

From the doorway, a veiled silhouette
of a beckoning woman
will welcome you in with *my dear*,
bring you *here* by the fire.
Gotten out of the wind, you can drop
what you gathered and carried,
secure in your favorite chair.
Then you toast her with wine
at the table; *try this*, the roast pork.
Fill your glass without asking,
give thanks as you should, make an offer
of wood, be at ease:

I am pleased, says the keeper of hearths,
who kept brothers and sisters
before they descended from mountains,
who came to this temple
you built with the promise of shelter,

who brought you inside.

Let Sleeping Dogs

His mistress belays the leash no longer.
He heels by himself. *Let sleeping dogs*,
she said once, aware he won't wander
or flee too far, certain the scents
he tracked before can't attract him to stray

after heats of strange bitches, to run
swift again, paws twitching, but

wake on the hearth of her woodburning stove.
Drawn from the streets, let sleeping dogs
in to figments and scraps, fart and scratch
without watch or ward, scolding or collar.
No mistress belays a longer leash.

Berry Picking

How lucky me with lucky you,
when summer solstice warmed our days,
to go to berry pick and graze
on blackcaps ripe in happy June.

Along the mapless paths we flew
with empty pails, and followed ways
of lucky me with lucky you,
when summer solstice warmed our days.

We found our fill of thorns and fruit
where tangled, brambly hedges raised
both blood and berry juice to taste.
This happy bounty picked by two
was lucky me with lucky you.

Perennials

First crocus
daffodil lilac in succession
dogwood buttercup bridal wreath iris
and iris again
star of bethlehem ground ivy
strawberry tulip and honeysuckle
then multiflora profuses and azalea shoots
with morning glory violets
day lilly bursts and peony clusters.

If you were Gaia,
it might look like fireworks on your skin.
If you were a rose
and I loomed above you,
it might resemble a local version
of some immarblized colossus.
If I picked you in your season
and we lay in this rocky bed,
we might appear perennial.

II.   The Randomly Spared

In the Aftermath,

even your winds all hold their breath, astounded
now by trunks and limbs you felled with ease
in sudden wrath. These canopies brought to ground
attest: your tantrums smite the tallest trees
(and those just blessed). If Quercus dared to stand
above the diabetic maples, climbed
with hubris overlooks that crown the land
– and paid, what was this skinny sapling's crime,
you crushed with wooden rain? It must have sinned
in undergrowth to draw such vengeful power.
Still, your steward here, whose words offend,
who faced the gales and screamed *Take me, you coward!*,
lives. While higher plans excuse the worst
of winds, the randomly spared inherit earth.

Wine of Wrath

Bells ring
in the wrong
year. Parts of 1932 appear.
Maybe the sun set a rung
lower down on some ladder,
lower down and cloudier.
The pay phone rang and rang
until you picked it up, connected,
and it's John Steinbeck:
Is Tom there?

No, wait. Throw the wine away.
Now it all comes back –
it's the church bells in chime.
Your head throbs, dissonant.
The Salvation Army kitchen
is open for the day,
and you've lost your place in line.

Cacophony in Concert

On stage, we were no ensemble,
filling the chairs like we were
and percussing under our breath.

A row of violence fiddled;
oompah-pah farted the tube
as the harpy was coming unstrung.

The oboys were back in the corner,
texting the saxes on phones
that some brassy strumpet was hot.

Offkeys of the keyboard were hammered;
notes of their discords kept time
to the bass jello's case of the shakes.

Outdinned by the clash of simples,
dums de-dumming offbeat,
I played the lead buffoon.

The conductor waved his baton,
so we waved back to him.
None of us knew the score;
tone-deaf to the chorus of boos.

A Mug's Argument

I say that all my friends are doing it;
the magic somehow turns my wrongs to right
and childhood alibis still work for real.
Each time I don't confess and don't admit
to hiding in a crowd that way, it might
be this mug's argument, but does appeal.

They caught me skipping school, and my appeal
was saying all my friends were doing it,
like running with my crowd that way just might
avoid the fact detention served me right.
The streets were not a school, but they'd admit
a wayward boy and teach me what was real.

And as for consequences, what was real
for me was consequences don't appeal.
So when you cheat or steal, just don't admit
your guilt, say all your friends are doing it.
I learned to duck, to bob and weave, and right
on up I climbed, not caring how I might.

From minor cons, ambition led and might
have made the man; the man became a real
chameleon, his colors always right.
A siren sang to me, her sly appeal
suggested all my friends were doing it;
the "it" that none would speak of or admit.

My talent grew to what I must admit
belonged in higher office, where I might
get fat like all my friends were doing it.
In my campaign, the slogan "keep it real"
would buy me votes; whatever words appeal.
To win was just my destiny, my right.

So now it's my vote up for sale, and right
along with drinks and dinners, bids admit
each bidder to my office with appeals.
And inside trades won't do, until they might,
though never fear, I won't be tried for real.
My plea is all my friends were doing it.

When it can turn my wrongs to right, I might
admit that this mug's argument has real
appeal. And all my friends are doing it.

Bourbon and Bienville

Here is the richly silted mud
from Mississippi's bed.
Here are deposits left by floods
in living silhouette.

Here are the convicts once paroled
as settlers to transport.
Here are the bodies cheaply sold
for labor or for sport.

Here is the gumbo's human spice
so many hands have stirred.
Here are the po-boys, beans and rice,
though beggars won't be served.

Here are the latest loud roués,
whose cries disturb your sleep.
Here is this morning's fresh bouquet
of vomit in the street.

Here are the blues from beaten drums
that hoodoo up your nape.
Here are the lines you have to hum,
the foot that always taps.

Here is the richly silted mud,
the dark deposits in your blood.

A Service Economy

Just in: on breaking TV news I hear
the cops have busted human traffic rings.
Offscreen, there's way more pimps than hookers here.

Authorities mixed up their perps, I fear,
with John Doe names on warrants for the sting.
Just in: on breaking TV news I hear

no news of brokers who so deftly clear
their fees, that age-old service economy thing.
All clean, the way more pimps than hookers here

can look legit on tax returns each year
without an inventory, businessing.
Just in: on breaking TV news I hear

no news that all our goods are made by mere
kids in Honduras, Seoul, Hong Kong, Beijing –
this way, there's more for pimps than hookers here.

Rings of consultants, factors, financiers
all favor *outsource* over *trafficking*.
Just in: on breaking TV news I hear
the spiels. There's way more pimps than hookers here.

At the Museum of the Book

Now folks, the first exhibit is a book,
the docent droned, that only we can touch
with latex gloves. So be content to look.

(Librarians had no one left to hush;
now this museum occupies their space.
The stacks are closed, and research pretty much.)

We think that size and format once were based
on folds in hand-laid sheets, producing leaves.
These letters, inked with type, would fill each face.

(Though others left us lessons to retrieve,
who'd bother reading shelves of printed texts?
So, here they're safe from all us oafs and thieves.)

Please move along; these glassed-in artifacts
are cordoned off. The printing press is next.

What It Is

is just a random string of lines, all full of
edgy tropes, not totally composed
and *dénouement* is dead, no more indulged.

It's music now disdained for tone deaf prose
and edgy tropes, a total decomposed.

Just keep it real to sounds of claquing hands
with music now disdained, for tone deaf prose
sees only grains of sand in grains of sand.
It keeps it real, but sounds of claquing hands,
vignettes of lush detail and sheer descript
seem only piles of sand from grains of sand.

Footless and fancy free they crow, those cryptic,
vain vignettes, details and sheer descript,
so solely I me my but nothing greater.

Footless and fancy free they cry in cryptic
reference, unmargined use of paper,
confessing I me my. There's nothing greater,
now *dénouement* is dead. With more indulged
self-reference, unmargined use of paper,
it's just a random string of lines, all full of

They're Not Wearing Capes

– For all the nurses in the 2020 pandemic.

They're wearing scrubs, the ones who hold the field.
They aren't armed with lightning bolt or shield;
in place of superhero cape, a gown.
But still they tend the stricken, broken-down,
contagious sick, until they're lost or healed.

Now Superman was given strength to wield,
the Flash was fast and Batman was well-heeled,
but what's the superpower, BAM! and POW!
of wearing scrubs?

And wouldn't even superheroes yield,
then run from viral villains all concealed
in us, if saving lives could risk their own?
The comic books can't match what's only shown
by those not made immortal or of steel,
just wearing scrubs.

As He Is to Us

Wiry and worn, well-tanned from the task,
the gravedigger goes to his goodly works
with a practiced pace, pick and spade.
On a slope commanding a modest meadow,
he's put in a potter's field of his pets;
a flock with fates more fleeting than his,
ones at his mercy, his will and mood.

Rocks and roots must be cleared from the clay,
so he digs deeper, then dutifully fills
with the burden he buries, barrow he tamps.
What's hard on the hands frees up the head;
prayers need replies, regrets must be purged
by he who decides when suffering stops.
Aloft or aground, God is alone.

Lights on the Dashboard

We once had muscle, shiny trim,
when racing engines drove our miles
on perfect bodies, stainless rims.
No dashboard lights for juveniles.

Those racing engines drove our miles
through signs and signals always green.
No dashboard lights for juveniles;
you ran like new, I <u>liked</u> eighteen.

Though signs and signals had been green,
there came the warnings, flickered red.
No longer new or like eighteen,
you needed oil, I sometimes bled.

There were the warnings, solid red,
but we ignored them, pressing on.
You needed oil, I often bled;
your tires grew bald, my hair half gone.

We still ignore them, pressing on.
More lights turn red behind your wheel;
your tires are bald, my hair is gone.
The doctors treat but cannot heal

the lights all red behind the wheel.
They won't go out, they just look back;
mechanics patch, but cannot heal.
The road becomes a cul-de-sac

with no way out but looking back
from broke-down bodies, rusted rims.
The road may be a cul-de-sac,
but we had muscle, shiny trim.

Once and Future Kings

I woke today to chirped and warbled sounds
of birds, but couldn't understand their tongue.
Perhaps they merely called a mate on down

to share some secret nest, to hatch their young,
or warned an interloping squirrel away;
You trespass in my woods, they might have sung.

But if their calls were meant for me, they'd say
they're rightful heirs of tyrant lizard lords,
too-whitt-ing auspices in ancient lays,

recalling times a thunderous tread towards
a hidden den made tiny mammals quail;
the times before the monkeys came in hordes

to walk the other way along this trail.
And those who traded fight for flight of wings
are waiting out the latest king to fail

while roosting on a lower branch to sing,
so clear: *the King is dead; long live the King*.

The Boomer Is Put Out to Pasture

It was when the world no longer wanted
Boomer (apparently past his prime)
that he lost his purpose, but looked at his land

and knew it needed a caretaker's keeping.
Starting again, he would spend himself
as if not apparently past his prime

in the causes of pruning, cutting and clearing,
mowing the milkweed and thistle to thatch.
This starting again, spending himself

as if hired at home by the hour, was work
(but was it like work, paying him wages?).
Mowing the milkweed and thistle to thatch,

or seasoning, splitting and stacking for fires,
offered what office or cubicle could;
for it was like work, paying him wages

– satisfied soreness of sinews and back.
And so when the world no longer wanted,
it offered what office or cubicle couldn't;
lost in his purpose, he looks to the land.

Other Structures

Near a nameless, forgotten graveyard,
where cornels encroach on toppled crosses
and spring from the sunken, fertile spots,
lingers what's left of a sturdy structure.
An aged barn, braced and embanked,
its siding resigned to warp, wearily
leans from level, needing a little
more than paint or plywood patches.
Its gutters are gone, done conducting
the runoff of standing seams (whose screws
were lost or lifted loose by prevailing
vandals). Varmints have holed the very
foundations down where the mortar dropped
from stone. Still, it's a home of humble
cover for bats and some cagey cats.
Closer, it's clear its beams bear
no signs they're sawn or quartered (while sundry
mills and men with mules were neighbors
then) – a thousand adze-marks, though.
These notches were hewn, but not for here,
and a mortise not tied to a tenon tells
of bygone use, beams bearing
lapse, collapse and salvage to serve
embedded as bones of a structure reborn.

III. Stories That Mothers Tell

"The mass of men lead lives of quiet desperation."

– H. Thoreau, *Walden* 1, *Economy*.

Stories That Mothers Tell

You know the stories that mothers tell
their crying children, of children
starving in [fill in the name of a country].
This isn't one of those stories.
No mother would ever quiet her child
with a story of losing reasons
like childhood friends, gracelessly growing
tired or just too rigid,
senses deserting you, breath by breath.
No, child, this isn't
one of the stories that mothers tell,
and as long as it isn't telling,
it quiets you.

Cinderella in Reverse

Once upon Cinderella, princess plum in
daddy's castle, met her prince at the ball
and wed, rode off in his sporty, five-speed pumpkin
(horseless) to his cul-de-sac manor hall.

After happily ever, she's the drudge
in his domain. Her shrewish mother-in-law's
no fairy, prince is gone in battle too much,
so Cinderella sings to mice, does laundry.

After happily ever, clocks strike twelve.
Now Cinderella's slippers aren't glass,
her fraying robe no gown. For magic itself
to be reversed, she'll need new spells to cast

new roles. She reads his daughters once upon
her backward tale, dispels a classic con.

The Clepsydra

Its inflow, outflow run on tears. Relentless
dripping times the hours to irrigate
your fields. It marks no lines of why, just when

to sprout and blossom in this place, to mate
and sow your own, to know the numbing frost,
become the harvest. Days that will not wait,

that weep from ducts, from spigots on or off,
evaporate. And all the while what's in
this fluid thief will count your seasons lost

downstream. It runs brim high with tears to spin
the solemn calendar of skies and skylings,
draining years. Too slowly you begin

to savor time in salty water flying
fleet through this machine, to stop the crying.

You Don't Know What You Don't Know

Once, when the sure and certain concealed
that ceilings were far from floors,
standing up straight by the jamb of a door
with the pencilled-in marks of my growth,
I towered and topped a mark or two.
Back in the day, I just knew

marks that reckoned my reach heroic,
not knowing the gauge of greatness
or useful units of height and weight.
Thus, in such wide-eyed wisdom,
ascent was assumed, scaled to my tools.
I measured by matching a ruler
when a yardstick surely served my cause,
not knowing what a yardstick was.

They're Here to Protect You
(From the Bogeyman)

The Bogeyman will get you if he can;
at least, that's what they say. If so, perchance
he lies in wait, he loiters under beds,
he haunts the closet next. Your lurking dread
awakes on cue, is running loose again.

They tell you, when the lights are out, he plans
to do you harm, then hide in ways you can't.
He'll jump you from behind, his cloak outspread,
that Bogeyman!

That's what they said, creating new demand
from scary tales. They'll offer now to ban
the conjured childhood monster they have fed
– for modest fees (they have their overhead).
And you? You'll pay until you understand
the Bogeyman.

Company Calling

Here in this dwelling, doorways lack doors.
No knocking announces the need to enter,
visitors vacate with nothing to close.
Those who abide for a bed and board
surrender rooms when rested and fed.
Some come to work, while there are wages,
and others who steal inside from storms
venture eventually out again.
Call these callers acquaintances, colleagues,
fellow sufferers, surely no more.

Those who remain when meals are at end,
beds are stripped bare, business is finished
and storms are all still – stayed not by doors,
only your company – call them friends.

For Lady Macbeth, in the 21st Century

We know the dirt you couldn't clean
with all your scrubbing, all your might;
the things that still are kept unseen.
These shadows trail us, not contrite
but wearing spotless alibis.
They come in darkness, make demands,
then disappear upon first light.
This is the way we wash our hands

of awkward disconnects between
a public face and appetites.
On stage, our poses strut and preen;
tell wordless lies that aren't white.
The viral buzz of this is quite
enough to launch our trending brands,
and dressed-up dirt is sanitized.
This is the way we wash our hands

of how we play Act Five, first scene,
where avatars deny, deny
(we'll hide behind a glowing screen),
and rage at every dirty slight
(in person, being more polite);
the anti-social network dance
with OCD knows no respite.
This is the way we wash our hands

of stories cleaner to rewrite
and sleepwalk through our spotless lands,
surrounded by these acolytes.
This is the way we wash our hands.

Life as a Boneless Chicken

Don't go all headless in Chicken Little mode
when falling acorns must be falling sky.
Don't count your chickens before they cross the road,

just think what feathers on the shoulders bode
and read the *billions and billions served* on signs.
Don't mourn the headless in Chicken Little mode

or beat your breast for all the yolks that flowed,
that never got a chance as wings or thighs.
Don't count on chickens, before they cross the road,

to tell the King. No cars or trucks are slowed
by crossers crawling for lack of bones or spines;
they're rendered headless in Chicken Little mode,

from carrion to carryout, a load
of freshly processed meat in nuggets, fried.
You'll count no chickens before they cross the road

when told to run and panic's being sowed.
They say the King is on the other side,
so go all headless in Chicken Little mode
like countless chickens before you – cross the road.

What Daughters Do

What daughters do, with charms that soon endear,
is wrap you round their fingers. Though you swear
to make them toe the line, you can't deny
the pull of pouted lip or teary eye.
But what they do won't stay at home, or near.

So it's no longer just your daughters here,
and on the evening news they can appear
as any girl; a face that's freckled by
what daughters do.

And now it's not just yours for whom you fear,
but all the ones abused or disappeared,
the ones who run, the ones too scared to try,
the ones who go too soon, without goodbye,
whose fingers you'll be wrapped around; it's clear
what daughters do.

Too Beautiful to Go to the Dance

Princess you've been
hours primping and preening,
already from the bath
wafts every exotic scent
of lotion and balm
brought for you from the east
by camel and caravan,
so take care you don't become
too beautiful,
for the light of your mirror
will go dark and give up,
unable to do you justice,
jewelry and other adornments
retreat to their drawers unworthy,
the makeup ashamed to cover your face,
the palace gates refuse to release
their embrace upon *open sesame*,
and the king who once ruled here
will see this great beauty
and be sore afraid
to let you go out to the dance
and the boy who awaits you.

My Son's Waltz (After Roethke)

I whirled you out of breath,
 a son made young, now dizzy.
We waltzed me back from death;
you made the choice seem easy.

(My good eye, still it panned
to bottles on the shelf,
where once it countenanced
a whiskeyed end itself.)

Each track that lined my wrist,
each rough and calloused knuckle,
said love was veins I missed
and knees that do not buckle.

Then music in my head
that danced us over dirt
said waltz you off to bed.
Your blanket was my shirt.

Just a Rondeau for Cassandra

I told you so, but do you listen? No!
As teenage sons look down at screens, she scolds
them both, appealing to the sides of heads
where earbuds go. Cassandra's words instead
are bouncing off, fall mute somehow. *Hello?*

You'll bring a girl and trouble home – I know!
Her warnings meet with sighs, the eyes that roll,
the mocking mimes behind her. Just forget
I told you so.

Their wooden horses wait – they have to go.
They'll text or post, of course, but can't be told
how tragic plays and epic losses get
replayed in repetends she sees ahead.
They've gone. Cassandra's left with this rondeau.
I told you so.

The Sentry

He stands alone, on duty here to man
his post, a shelf of books with dusty spines,
all full of old adventures, famous wars,
of light brigades and glory on the field.
His comrades, laid in boxes, waited once
to charge in rows and storm the valley floor
that ran across their general's room, in drills
commanded by the general after school,
until his mother called *It's time for bed.*

The sentry stands his watch, as ordered to,
his molded base enforcing discipline.
The room is quiet now, without the sound
effects of cannon shells or cheering troops.
Though all his comrades left, in boxes laid
to rest in landfills (none will charge again),
and new adventures led the general off
to other wars (where mother doesn't call
It's time for bed), the sentry guards this place.

The Telephone Game

The beacon moon is out, and shines on tangent.
Children merge from darkest woods, where there's
a clearing. Now we play the game again.

We form a circle, I whisper in your ear,
you pass it on to someone next to you:
In the beginning . . . Polaris dips to steer

amidst the clearing, murmurs circle and grow
and now we learn a lesson. Then, one after
another, playmates whisper, hearing no

thing new beneath the moon but slantly muttered
To be or not to be . . . Stars burn till dawn
in constellations, circles form. This cluster

of children in a clearing learns from only
moon and stars, each other. Now we ax
the nighttime woods with games of telephone

as whispers near and mouth to ear inflects.
A child close by repeats what he understands as
$E = MC^2$ . . . You whisper next.

Biographical Note

Poems have been coming to Ted Charnley since he was 17, beginning with the suicide of a high school classmate. Following careers in law and rare books, his verse has appeared in multiple issues of such journals as *The Orchards*, *The Road Not Taken*, *Think*, *The Lyric* and *Passager*, and in the recent anthology *Extreme Sonnets*. He lives with his wife in a 200-year-old farmhouse they restored in central Maryland. There, he herds woodchucks, practices chainsaw topiary and leaves offerings for the nymphs of the springs.

www.ingramcontent.com/pod-product-compliance
Lightning Source LLC
Chambersburg PA
CBHW031152090426
42738CB00008B/1301